GARDEN GNOMES
A HISTORY

Twigs

SHIRE PUBLICATIONS

Published in Great Britain in 2010 by Shire Publications
Ltd, Midland House, West Way, Botley, Oxford OX2 0PH,
United Kingdom.
44-02 23rd St, Suite 219, Long Island City,
NY 11101, USA.

E-mail: shire@shirebooks.co.uk   www.shirebooks.co.uk

© 2009 Twigs Way; reprinted 2010.

Every attempt has been made by the Publishers to secure
the appropriate permissions for materials reproduced in
this book. If there has been any oversight we will be happy
to rectify the situation and a written submission should be
made to the Publishers.

A CIP catalogue record for this book is available from the
British Library.

Shire Library no. 487   •   ISBN-13: 978 0 7478 0710 0

Twigs Way has asserted her right under the Copyright,
Designs and Patents Act, 1988, to be identified as the
author of this book.

Designed by Ken Vail Graphic Design, Cambridge, UK and
typeset in Perpetua and Gill Sans.
Printed in China through Worldprint Ltd.

10 11 12 13 14   11 10 9 8 7 6 5 4 3 2

COVER IMAGE
Catalogue of Ludwig Möller.

TITLE PAGE IMAGE
The laughing Gnome.

CONTENTS PAGE IMAGE
An assortment of gnomes on the balcony of a model
windmill.

ACKNOWLEDGEMENTS

I would like to thank the following for their generous help
in providing information, photographs and insight during
the writing of this short history. They all entered into the
spirit of the book with great enthusiasm. Anne Andrews,
Dorset Gardens Trust; Allan Brocklebank and Jim
Chadderton for the history of the Harcostar gnomes;
Michael Carden for the 'Walgrave gnome'; Rod Conlon for
information on the Stoke Park gnomes; Paul Crowther of
H. Crowther Ltd, who provided information and images
from the Crowther catalogue; Simon Dabell, Vectis
Ventures (Blackgang Chine, Isle of Wight); Brent Elliott,
librarian and archivist of the Royal Horticultural Society,
Lindley Library, who as ever gave generously of his
knowledge and kindly provided a copy of his own article on
'Gnomenclature'; Sue Gordon-Roe, who shared her
childhood gnome with me; Liz Hope of the
Northamptonshire Gardens Trust and her colleagues at the
Lamport Hall Preservation Trust; Brian Kibler for images
and information on Maresch gnomes; Candice Kimmel and
Richard Paul Kimmel of Kimmel Gnomes; Philip Norman
at the Museum of Garden History, Lambeth, for sharing the
Museum's collection of gnomes; Jane Preston, descendant
of the Bassett-Lowke family of Number 78 Derngate; Beth
Sanderson for sharing her gnome blog; Amoret Tanner for
ferreting out more gnome catalogues; and Andrew Widd,
head gardener at Friar Park, for treating my persistent
enquiries with great patience.

Photographs and illustrations are from the author's
collection except as follows, acknowledged with many
thanks, and where copyright is reserved:

Amoret Tanner Collection, pp. 14 (both), 16 (top), and
31 (bottom); Bedfordshire and Luton Archives Service,
pp. 8 (bottom left), 10 (both), 20 (all), and 21 (bottom);
Russell Butcher, contents page; Cambridge University
Library, Waddleton Collection, p. 17 (both); Michael
Carden p. 25 (top); Jim Chadderton p. 42; Paul
Crowther, p. 33 (both); Mary Evans Picture Gallery p. 32
(bottom); istockphoto.com pp. 8 (right), 9 (both), 30, 32
(top), 40 (top left), 41, 46 (top), and 55; Brian Kibler
pp. 11 (both), and 12; Kimmel Gnomes, pp. 47 (both),
and 48 (top); Lamport Hall Trust p. 22; Lindley Library,
Royal Horticultural Society, cover and pp. 6 and 15;
Museum of Garden History, pp. 5, 13, 16 (bottom), 24
(bottom), 26 (bottom), 28 (bottom), 37 (bottom left),
37 (bottom right), 38, 43 (top), 49 (bottom), 50, 51
(bottom), 53 (bottom); Oxfordshire County Council
pp. 25 (bottom) and 26 (top); Jane Preston and 78
Derngate p. 27; Science and Society Picture Library
pp. 18 and 24 (top).

Shire Publications is supporting the Woodland Trust, the UK's leading woodland conservation charity, by funding the dedication of trees.

CONTENTS

INTRODUCTION

ASK ANYONE to describe a garden gnome and you will receive a reply involving white beards, red hats, suburban lawns, and a selection of garden utensils including wheelbarrows, rakes and sometimes fishing gear. There may be a mention of the usually small size, an association with windmills, or a smiling remark on the modern trend towards 'under-dressed' gnomes. However, things have not always been as simple or definitions so easy. The term 'garden gnome' has a complex history needing some explanation, before the history of the gnomes themselves is tackled.

Northern Europe has a strong tradition of belief in 'little folk', with elves, leprechauns, dwarfs, *tomte* and other variants peopling the countryside. In Thuringia, the supposed birthland of the garden gnome, mythical red-jacketed dwarfs were said to recall actual miners, who arrived in prehistoric times from Crete. Whatever the size, origins, or nationality, the pointed red hat and tight jacket reflected the traditional uniform of mine workers in the area. The similarly attired *tomte* of Swedish folklore were also small, white-bearded figures who traditionally helped above ground in the stables and farms of agricultural Scandinavia, whilst the predominantly green leprechauns haunted the wild and historic sites of Ireland, trading as cobblers and tinkers. The Danish *nisse* was even associated with Santa Claus (sometimes referred to as the *Julenisse*).

At some point in their long folk history, the *tomte* and dwarfs of imagination took on a physical form and began to be represented by small figurines placed around the house and, eventually, the garden. In Sweden a single *tomte* was usual, whilst in Germany small groups were more common.

When first encountered by English tourists in the nineteenth century these were referred to as *Gnomen-Figuren*, although the figures themselves were actually dwarfs. Early catalogues from Germany selling what we would now call a garden gnome often specify the term *Zwergen-Figuren*. In England and America the term 'garden gnome' came to be associated with the figures with white beards and red hats from early on in their migration; their extraordinary physical similarity to the traditionally more gruff and unfriendly dwarf or the Swedish *tomte* was simply brushed aside.

To complicate matters further, a range of large garden figures known as *gobbi* or *Callot* figures appeared in Renaissance and eighteenth-century gardens in southern Europe, based on life-sized human dwarfs or grotesques. These appear to have given inspiration to the larger-scale garden gnomes of the later nineteenth century, whose size distinguishes them from their small northern European cousins, but whose clothing is markedly 'gnomish'. Thus the small figure that lurks in many a modern shrubbery and is readily described as a 'garden gnome' might more accurately be known as a garden dwarf or *Zwerge*, a *tomte* or even a *gobbi*.

Although this book might more properly be entitled 'miniature garden figures', (or 'dwarfs, *tomte*, *gobbi* and other figures'!) I have adhered to the better known and now established term 'garden gnomes', hoping thereby to encompass all gnomish ancestors.

A range of garden gnomes of all periods, styles and sizes, but each wearing the traditional red hat. These are part of the collection at the Museum of Garden History in London.

No. 933.

No. 934.

No. 946.

No. 941.

No. 942.

No. 930.

No. 935.

No. 932.

Preise der Gnomen aus dem Gartentechnischen Geschäft von Ludwig Möller in Erfurt.

No. 930. 80 cm hoch, 30 M. — No. 931. 67 cm hoch, 16 M. — No. 932. 89 cm hoch, 28 M. 50 Pf. — No. 933. 65 cm hoch, 23 M. 50 Pf. — No. 934. 70 c hoch, 23 M. 50 Pf. — No. 935. 65 cm hoch, 26 M. — No. 936. 65 cm hoch, 16 M. — No. 937. 52 cm hoch, 16 M. — No. 938. 95 cm hoch, 28 M. 50 P No. 939. 93 cm hoch, 28 M. 50 Pf. — No. 940. 96 cm lang, 28 M. 50 Pf. — No. 941. 70 cm lang, 16 M. — No. 942. 55 cm lang, 16 M. — No. 943. 68 c hoch, 16 M. — No. 944. 60 cm hoch, 16 M. — No. 945. 90 cm hoch, 26 M. — No. 946. 115 cm hoch, 60 M. — Verpackung billigst zum Selbstkostenprei

EARLY HISTORY AND EUROPEAN HOMELANDS

GARDEN GNOMES have their origins in the mists of time, when the elements of land, air and fire were each associated with their own spirit forms. Dwarfs, goblins, fairies, and other spirits haunted the world and could, it was said, be glimpsed or heard by those sensitive to their presence. In one of the first uses of the word, 'gnomes' were described by the sixteenth-century alchemist and physician, Paracelsus, as the 'shrews of the earth', responsible for geological activity as it was then understood. The geological link was restated by the poet and gardening guru Alexander Pope in his eighteenth-century work *The Rape of the Lock*, where he describes gnomes as 'Daemons of the Earth, who delight in mischief'. Erasmus Darwin in *The Botanic Garden* (1791) also gave gnomes dominion over the earth, teaching 'the volcanic airs to force through bubbling Lavas their resistless course'. For well-read English speakers, the term 'gnome' thus became familiar as a name for 'little folk' or elemental creatures who worked underground, controlling the elements of the earth itself.

The first garden figurines or statues that we might recognise as garden gnomes were, however, not based on these elementals, but instead on the more human dwarf. Statues and figures of gods, goddesses, naiads and fauns were common in Renaissance and baroque gardens of Europe, adding to the formal gardens a population of otherworldliness. *Gobbi* (as dwarfs and hunchbacks were known in Italy) also appeared amongst these classical figures, posing as musicians, beggars and comedy players. Jacques Callot in particular designed twenty-one *gobbi* pieces, designs that were engraved and printed in Florence in 1616 and subsequently widely distributed. Unlike later garden gnomes, these *Zwergen-Figuren* or *gobbi* did not dress in the typical pointed hat, nor carry tools of the mining trade, but instead posed as lovers, dancers and even a Turkish Pasha. These were dwarfs as part of the Italian *Commedia dell'arte* tradition rather than as the earthy spirits of the mine, dwarfs with culture and class rather than pickaxes and shovels. Seen in all the best gardens, the orchestra and lovers were present at Schloss Sinning (near Neuburg in Germany), and at the garden of the Prince Bishops at Augsburg.

Opposite:
Catalogues are all that remains of so many garden gnome manufacturers. This catalogue from Ludwig Möller depicts many hunting, shovelling, and drinking *Gnomen-Figuren*.

7

In the early eighteenth century, a series of engravings of dwarf statues circulated in Germany and Austria, based on the earlier designs by Callot. This resulted in the garden dwarf again becoming a popular figure of garden statuary in upper-class German gardens. Sitting comfortably alongside the grottoes and rock-work arbours that echo their elemental association, these dwarfs would sometimes be painted in bright colours, or given musical instruments to entertain through the long hours. In her examination of the Hofgarten at Oettingen (near Nördlingen in Germany), Countess Dohna traced the history of the series of dwarfish figures there from their origins in the seventeenth-century baroque garden on the site through to the modern day. Goethe also made reference to a garden decorated with 'figures of stone and the coloured dwarfs' in *Hermann and Dorothea* (1797).

A short story written by Adalbert Stifter in the 1840s refers to garden dwarfs as a form of garden nostalgia, harking back to their heyday of the eighteenth century. In his story the dwarfs are discovered in an old orchard, where 'around a well in the overgrown grass ... stood grey stone dwarfs with bagpipes, lyres, clarinets, and all sorts of musical instruments in their hands'. The grass is long, the paths overgrown, and the dwarfs stand unloved, unpainted and mutilated, testament to a time passed and a fashion long gone.

Eventually translated into smaller porcelain pieces and transferred into the house, these German garden figures forge a link between the garden dwarf of the Renaissance and the later garden gnome.

By the late eighteenth century, 'house dwarfs' of porcelain appear to have infiltrated both the German and the English market. In the 1780s Derby (later Crown Derby) was offering 'dwarfs' amongst its catalogue of collectable porcelains. The popular 'Mansion House Dwarf' design was based on real dwarfs who were hired to display advertising signs and stood outside

Below: The china cabinet at Hinwick Hall (Bedfordshire) with a single porcelain figure displayed. The figure was typical of several owned by Frederica Orlebar and other members of upper-class society in this period.

Below right: *Gobbi* or *Zwergen* figures such as these were once common in eighteenth-century German gardens. Often grouped like the later garden gnome, these examples survive in the gardens at Mirabel, Salzburg, Austria.

Far right: Early garden figures or gobbi included a range of 'grotesques' such as this Punch look-alike (Mirabel Gardens, Salzburg).

Right: Unlike the later garden dwarf, early eighteenth-century *gobbi* figures included women.

the Mansion House in London. The use of porcelain permitted their colourful clothing, despite the English preoccupation with 'taste'; all other materials necessitated muted, supposedly classical, colourings. The porcelain figures retained their popularity throughout the nineteenth century, decorating many a florid Victorian dining room. In the 1880s, for example, Frederica Orlebar of Bedfordshire kept a collection of such porcelain gnomes on her china shelf, and even wrote stories about their supposed adventures. In 1906 the magazine *The Connoisseur* included an article describing the porcelain collection of Lieutenant Colonel Powney, who had as many as twenty-two porcelain 'dwarfs'. *The Connoisseur* also carried advertisements for the porcelain figures produced by the German manufacturer Wahliss, later to become famous for its garden figures. It was almost certainly these ceramic charms that became the first garden gnomes in England, being imported initially as house ornaments and then placed in the garden. In both Germany and Switzerland gnomes (or dwarfs) also began to be made in white clay or terracotta; and used as good luck charms in the house, supplementing the finer porcelain.

In addition to these porcelain and terracotta figures, another class of popular dwarfish representations spread across Europe in the nineteenth century, further complicating the ancestry and descent of the garden gnome. The mountains and landscapes of Interlaken and Lucerne had long held dear the folklore of little people, including dwarfs who helped in the woods and mines. Wooden carvings were made of these dwarfs as well as other figures, to decorate the house. As the fashion for the picturesque drew

Victorian travellers to these landscapes and to their folklore, the figurines became fashionable. Soon wooden carvings of animals, chalets, figures, religious scenes and 'gnomes' (again in fact dwarfs) were being carved as mementoes for the burgeoning tourist industry. Despite being originally focused in the Swiss town of Brienz, these were known as Black Forest carvings, eventually spreading to Germany and Austria. Originally gracing just local houses, from the 1820s they became an export industry and hand-carved gnome/dwarfs flooded back to England in the bags of aristocratic travellers alongside the famous carved bears and the less popular nativity scenes. These wooden figurines were destined for indoors rather than the garden, where they joined the more colourful porcelain figures on mantelshelves and in display cabinets. Like the porcelain figures they came to be regarded as works of art and were exhibited in London at the Great Exhibition in 1851, in Chicago in 1893, and Paris in 1900.

The origins of the first ever purpose-made ceramic or terracotta garden gnome are hotly debated. The honour is frequently and variously claimed, as exact dates are hard to establish in the absence of catalogues (most of which did not appear until the later nineteenth century). Several of the companies that claim to be the creators of the first garden gnomes actually post-date the introduction of the earliest gnomes into English gardens, and so must have

In this earliest English collection of gnomes at Lamport Hall (Northamptonshire) most gnomes were miniatures, some 'on loan' from their indoor duties.

Inside the famous Maresch factory. A typically large gnome can be seen being painted by a standing female worker.

taken their designs and ideas from earlier manufacturers of the house gnomes. For a while indeed the two types of gnome must have existed side by side as tourists brought back all types of figures and placed them randomly in house or garden. The gnomes at the famous Lamport Hall in Northamptonshire (said to be the first collection of garden gnomes in the country and discussed in the next chapter) were almost all small 'house' gnomes, and comments made by Sir Charles Isham, the creator of the gnomery at Lamport, indicate that some had been pressed into service from other calls of duty, such as holders of dinner place-cards, boxes of matches, or ornaments in china cabinets.

Most of the early purpose-made garden gnomes were manufactured using terracotta clay slurry which was moulded and painted. Early moulds still survive in gnome museums in Germany and in the Museum of Garden History in London. Some manufacturers also used a fabric with a high ironstone content or 'thick red clay' (the latter appears to have been modelled rather than moulded).

Alfred Baehr and Johann Maresch have a strong claim to be the first ever manufacturers of ceramic garden gnomes. By 1841 Baehr owned a factory in Pirna near Dresden (Germany) producing gnomes amongst its other ceramic wares. Baehr was joined by Johann Maresch, and the two were partners until Baehr's death in 1849. The firm continued under the 'BM' logo as Maresch married Baehr's daughter, and traded as the Baehr and Maresch Siderolith Fabrik, based at Aussig an der Elbe, presumably continuing with gnome production. From 1863 they developed a worldwide trade, using the famous 'JM' logo. Baehr and Maresch used an ironstone clay mix to produce a more durable material, making their figurines suitable for both indoor and outdoor use. Under Johann's son, Ferdinand, the business prospered and gnomes and other ceramic decorative pieces were shipped to Europe and America, probably including some of the gnomes bought by Sir Frank Crisp for Friar

Johann Maresch, father of the Maresch gnomes.

A Maresch catalogue of the early 1900s. The gnomes here appear small but many were 3 feet tall, whilst the human figures might be life size.

Park, an early gnome garden in Oxfordshire. These Maresch figures were often large, some 2 to 3 feet in height, reminiscent of the size of the Renaissance *gobbi* figures but with the unmistakable features of the traditional dwarf/gnome. At the outbreak of war in 1939 production ceased, and Ferdinand Maresch died in 1940. A brief revival after the war was centred on production of the busts of the new communist president, rather than gnomes, but this was not a success and closure followed.

By the 1860s the firm of Eckardt and Mentz had also started to make ceramic gnomes. Very little is known of this firm, but a catalogue of the 1920s shows gnomes of high quality with detailed modelling and facial features. Some are illustrated with attached planters and palms, which might suggest an indoor location, perhaps within a conservatory or winter garden. In common with so many of the German factories, Eckardt and Mentz closed in the 1940s.

August Heissner is one of the best-known names in garden gnomes. Heissner manufactured his first garden gnome at a factory in Gräfenroda (Thuringia, Germany) in 1872, giving rise to the claim that Gräfenroda was the birthplace of the gnome – not least by the local tourist board! The ceramic gnomes were made in moulds, and after firing they were lovingly hand painted in the same reds and blues that are so well known today. By now the *Zwergen-Figuren* had taken on the standard appearance recognisable as that of the 'traditional' garden gnome, and far removed from that of the original Renaissance *gobbi* or *Callot* figures, or even the Crown Derby porcelains.

Also based in Gräfenroda, the Griebel family had founded a ceramics manufactory in the 1860s, making terracotta animals as decorations for both house and garden. In 1880 Philipp Griebel created and marketed the first of the Griebel garden gnome figures for which he and his company were to become famous. The Griebel family continued to manufacture gnomes through the nineteenth century and, with a short break for the Second World War, up to the current day, even introducing the first female gnome in the 1960s.

Early garden gnomes were created using moulds such as this one, which survives in the Museum of Garden History, London.

The creation of East Germany, including within it Thuringia, gave an impetus to the *Garten zwergmanufactur* as the gnomes became a successful and cheaply made export to Western Germany and other parts of Europe. This success also resulted in rivals, as manufacturers such as Louis Romeiss also set up in Gräfenroda. The Romeiss gnomes, now very rare, were made in earthenware and were known for their outstanding detail in the modelling and painting. Standing about a foot tall they are highly sought-after by gnome collectors. In addition to Griebel and Romeiss there were once sixteen gnome manufacturers in Gräfenroda, a testimony to the popularity of the gnome in the late nineteenth and early twentieth century.

A catalogue of the early 1900s from the Heissner collection. The gnomes are shown fishing and barrowing in a typically mountainous landscape. The catalogue is entitled 'Fairyland' and included animals as well as gnomes.

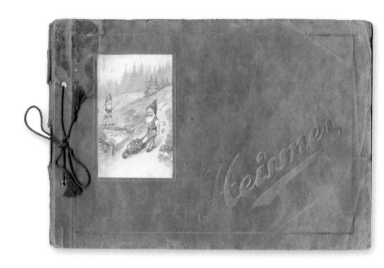

A page from the Heissner catalogue. This shows garden gnomes in typical stances, but on other pages miniatures are shown as menu holders, vases and even pencil-sharpeners.

At the time that the Griebels were advertising terracotta gnomes, brightly coloured porcelain indoor gnomes were rivalling them in the European and English market. In the middle of the nineteenth century Ernst Wahliss founded a new porcelain company in the Czech Republic, trading eventually throughout Europe, with stores in Vienna and London. Coming from the central European heartland of the dwarf, the Wahliss family saw the appeal of their figures as outdoor as well as indoor decoration. Wahliss's sons went on to buy up the original moulds for the porcelains of the former Imperial and Royal Porcelain Manufactory in Vienna in the 1890s, amongst which must also have been dwarfish figurines. In October 1908 Wahliss included in their usual advertisement in *The Connoisseur* magazine 'Gnomes and quaint manikins, which we stock in all styles and sizes lend[ing] themselves particularly well for the artistic decoration of parks and gardens etc'. The company went on to state that one of their clients already had over a hundred of these in his famous subterranean passages and gardens, a claim that suggests they had been trading in the figurines for some time. The famous client was probably Charles Isham at Lamport Hall, although Sir Frank Crisp at Friar Park has

A page from a Ludwig Möller catalogue, including 'gnome with rabbit', which was to become a popular sentimental figure in twentieth-century suburban gardens.

This delightful colour page from an early Heissner catalogue includes a series of scenarios including the card players, which we will see later on the Isle of Wight.

A fine gnome of about 1900, with fishing rod in hand. Note the sandals on this model, which appear very similar to the modern fashionable 'Birkenstock'.

also been suggested as the mystery client. These Wahliss gnomes were of a different quality and appearance to the ceramic, 'cement' or stone gnomes made by many of the companies specifically for garden use, although the ironstone ceramics of the Maresch factory were of a cross-over type of reinforced porcelain, with ironstone adding strength.

Outside Gräfenroda, the manufacture of gnomes spread first through central Europe and then across to America and England. The Bernard Bloch manufactory, originally of Bohemia (now within the Czech Republic) produced gnomes from the 1870s onwards, with pieces signed with the trademark 'BB'. Its company operated under the Bernard Bloch name until 1940, when it became Eichwald Porcelain and Stove Factory Bloch & Co. It was nationalized in 1945. Its products varied from miniatures of a few inches high to standing pieces of a foot or more. The highly coloured work of the Bloch gnome is typical of porcelain figures in its detail, but identical to the garden gnome in its clothing and appearance.

Gnomes (or *Gartenfiguren*) entered what was optimistically described as 'a new era' when C. F. Ortlebb created his *Moderne Gartenfiguren* for *Kunstgewerbe* (crafts) in the early 1900s. Here were gnomes not 'in the round' but in the flat. Ortlebb's gnomes appear to have been manufactured from tin or another flat metal, and painted with waterproof oils for weatherproofing. Fixed to the ground by a built-in stake, they could be accompanied by various signs including: 'Walking Here is Forbidden', 'Stop for Coffee' and 'Fresh Roses'. Alternatively, those with no services (or restrictions) to offer might purchase companions for their gnomes including a group of rabbits (with or without clothes), herons, or a Little Red Riding Hood. Unfortunately the designs are numbered rather than titled, so there is no record of whether these were thought of as *Zwergen* or gnomes.

At first America lagged behind Europe in gnome manufacture and enthusiasm. The Silvestri family was amongst the first to manufacture gnomes in America. Arcangelo Silvestri moved to San Francisco from Tuscany in about 1900, where his successful statuary company included ornamental mouldings and figurines. Returning to Tuscany during the great depression, Arcangelo's son and grandson came back to San Francisco in 1956, founding the A. Silvestri Company Fine Statuary, which included gnomes within its figurines. The company still makes garden gnomes in a distinctive cast stone with fine detailing.

The front of the Ortlebb catalogue of modern garden figures. Ortlebb was based in Thuringia, the heartland of the traditional gnome.

Few other companies survived into the twenty-first century, although Griebel and Heissner are still making gnomes amongst their other garden ornaments. Many of the manufacturers closed down during the difficult war years, or during the subsequent communist era in East Germany when trade was restricted. The association between the gnome and Germany may also have been partly to blame for the fall from fashion of the garden gnomes in England after the First World War.

The 'new era' gnomes were highly coloured, and the two dimensions made the inclusion of detail and accessories much easier.

THE STATELY GNOME: GNOMES GAIN A FOOTHOLD IN ENGLAND

THE JOURNEY of the gnome from its original homelands in central Europe to the quietude of the English stately garden, and its subsequent gradual transformation to the cheeky garden gnome of suburbia, was a journey initiated by Sir Charles Isham (1809–1903). Inheriting the estate of Lamport Hall (Northamptonshire) in 1846 following the suicide of his brother Justinian, Sir Charles rapidly gained a reputation for eccentricity. Spiritualist, teetotaller, vegetarian, non-smoker and hater of all blood sports, Sir Charles fitted uneasily, if at all, into Victorian aristocracy. His happy marriage and benevolence towards his employees was typical of a life spent in pursuit of poetry rather than pheasants. Horticulture was one of Sir Charles's greatest loves, and he created the largest north-facing Alpine garden known in England at the time. He commenced the rockery at Lamport Hall in 1847. Sited close to the house and forming what *Country Life* was later to describe as 'a disconcerting eruption'. Its closeness was mainly due to the enthusiasm of its creator, who wanted to be able to access the rockery easily and rapidly at all times of day and night as it was the focus of his horticultural endeavours.

Described in *The Strand Magazine* as 30 yards long by 14 yards wide and 8 yards high, the rockery had an ivy-covered sheer wall turned south towards the lawns, whilst the Alpine aspect faced north. Here were the crevices, chasms, caves and shoulders of rock that echoed the real Alps. Sir Charles undertook the planting of these rocks with great care, and although the collection was not of great variety the intention was to have everything in proportion within the miniaturised scale. Dwarf conifers, Japanese maples, box, and ferns, formed a background for purple thymes, golden saxifrage and lavender. The use of dwarf trees in rockeries had been noted in John Claudius Loudon's influential *Encyclopaedia of Gardening*, a book that every serious gardener of the period owned. Charles Isham made specific mention of this in a later pamphlet which he variously entitled '*Remarks on Rock Gardens and Notes on Gnomes*' or '*Notes on Gnomes and Remarks on Rock Gardens*'.

Sir Charles had obviously been disappointed by the endeavours of other rock garden enthusiasts, as he comments, 'The Rock Garden, so charming in

Opposite:
*Old Familiar
Flowers.* A 1919
autochrome
photograph by Mrs
G. A. Barton.

Above: Sir Charles Isham in his later years. An illustration accompanying a poem to his wife in which he declared that since her death his rockery had been his main consolation.

Above right: The front cover of *Notes on Gnomes and Remarks on Rock Gardens* showing Sir Charles's lettering. The word 'Gnomes' spreads across the whole page.

Right: The beautifully produced pamphlet written by Sir Charles Isham in which he remarks that gnomes 'would not have been admitted into the Lamport Hall Rockery' if they had only been imaginary creations but as there is much evidence for their existence they are not things of mental delusion but rather 'Extension of Faculty'.

anticipation, usually so disappointing in result, is well suited to the climate.' He emphasised the need to replicate nature, declaring that although he had had the opportunity to include 'druid stones' he had refrained from doing so for fear of vulgarising the site by introducing modern antiquity. Instead he introduced a large number of gnomes in this miniature landscape, which he claimed gave it its 'chief attraction' and 'most characteristic feature'. Had gnomes been imaginary creations however, he states firmly he would not have permitted them onto the Lamport Rockery.

Sir Charles must have first encountered gnomes in his extensive reading on folklore. He regularly holidayed in North Wales, where tales of little blacksmiths and gnomish miners echoed those on the continent. He soon

The rockery at Lamport Hall still survives. This is the front of the rockery, which faced Sir Charles's bedroom and is only a few feet from the house.

began to collect stories of gnomes and 'mine fairies' from Wales, Dovedale (England), Germany, Bohemia, and Hungary. These small folk, he claimed, should be regarded not as 'an indication of mental delusion but rather an extension of faculty'. Belief in the existence of fairies was a part of Sir Charles's spiritualism, but what induced him to place these figures in his rockery?

In 1613, Giovanni Battista Andreini had published a work called *L'Adamo*, which included an illustration of the possible appearance of the Garden of Eden. This contained a small figure placed within a rocky garden. This same

The Lamport Hall gnomes pictured in the *Gardeners' Chronicle* in 1897. This tableau included a sign demanding better working conditions – perhaps a forerunner of the modern Gnome Liberation Front?

woodcut was then reproduced by John Claudius Loudon in his *Encyclopaedia of Gardening*. Although not actually depicting gnomes, this did give an inspiration for figures in a miniature garden landscape. Sir Charles refers to pictures in Loudon's book and the miniaturisation of conifers as providing him with the idea of small figures in amongst the 'pygmy garden'. Whatever played the major part in starting his collection, spiritualism or gardening, Sir Charles would have had ample opportunity to purchase his gnomes on his travels to central Europe.

As the rockery – or gnomery – at Lamport Hall developed, caverns and tunnels were created with groups of gnomes in them, along with a 'Crystal Cavern'. Gnomes mined the crevices, climbed down ladders, shouldered their work tools, or paused for refreshments. Brought over especially from Germany, probably including the work of the manufacturer Wahliss, numerous gnomes inhabited the rockery by the end of Charles Isham's life. Liberated from what he regarded as their inappropriate housing in drawing rooms, they were grouped into outdoor tableaux. Posed around ladders and wells, and provided with miniature tools, they lived a rugged outdoor existence harking back to their mining origins; some were even provided with banners proclaiming the need for a decent wage and a benevolent employer, another of Isham's preoccupations. As Sir Charles said, they were 'more at home standing listlessly [on strike] at the mouth of the pit than supporting a dinner card as intended.'

The rockery was featured in the horticultural periodical *Gardeners' Chronicle* in 1897 and the prestigious *Country Life* in 1898, which undoubtedly did much to popularise the figures. *The Strand Magazine* found the gnomes charming and declared that they 'closely harmonised with each other, and produce a life-like effect, which was first conceived by the constructor and afterwards worked out with such skilful care'; whilst the *Gardeners' Chronicle* stated that 'the pretty miniature figures … increase the weirdness and novelty of the scene'. Although the gnomes at Lamport Hall varied in size, most were quite miniature, only 2 or 3 inches tall, and thus designed to be in keeping with the dwarf conifers and alpine plants with which they shared their rockery. They were accompanied in some cases by inscriptions, including one that hints at numerous visitors to the famous rockery, leaving its reclusive owner 'too kind to complain, yet he doubtless alone would prefer to remain'. Even the prestigious creators of rock gardens to the aristocracy, James Backhouse

'Lampy' is the only gnome surviving from the original gnome collection of Sir Charles Isham. Perhaps the most famous garden gnome in the world, he is currently insured for £1 million and only leaves his secure indoor residence to attend gnome conventions.

& Sons, described the Lamport Hall rockery as being the most impressive they had ever seen: 'It is, in fact, difficult to describe, so perfect is the illusion.' (Incidentally, Backhouse did not mention the gnomes.)

Modern replacements are now used in the Lamport Hall Rockery, and facsimiles of Lampy can be purchased in the gift shop.

After Sir Charles's death the gnomes were banished by his daughters and only one now survives. 'Lampy', perhaps the most famous gnome in the world, is on show to curious visitors who are assured that he is indeed insured for over £1 million. Recently called upon to attend a gnome convention in New Zealand, Lampy now lives in a secure glass case indoors – a curious end for a small gnome from Nuremburg.

In 1970 the ex-Beatle George Harrison was photographed for the cover of his new album *All Things Must Pass* with a collection of garden gnomes. The gnomes were inhabitants of Harrison's country estate of Friar Park, Oxfordshire, and had belonged to the original owner, Sir Frank Crisp. Like Sir Charles Isham, Crisp was regarded by many of his contemporaries as a bit of an eccentric. Commissioning the 120-room house in Gothic revival style in 1896, Sir Frank had surrounded the house with an array of gardens: a Dutch garden, an Elizabethan-style garden, a Nosegay garden, a Boccaccio garden and a 'Marian' garden, stocked with plants associated with the Virgin Mary. Taking the Victorian fashion for rockery building to extremes, he also constructed an enormous rockery centred on a scale model of the Matterhorn almost 30 feet high. Containing three caverns, the miniature mountain also had model (tin) chamois grazing its slopes. Within this rockery there was a maze of chambers and caves connected by an underground stream.

Sir Frank Crisp, lawyer, botanist and eccentric. He was the owner of Friar Park.

Sir Frank was a serious horticulturalist and member of the Linnean Society, specialising rather predictably in alpine plants. His skills were complimented in the Linnean Society by distinguished horticulturalists such as Gertrude Jekyll and Professor Henri Correvon. In 1919 he was awarded the Victoria Medal of the Royal Horticultural Society, although the RHS was notably quiet on the subject of his gnomes. The gnomes themselves did not have a quiet life, however, but appear to have been stolen or sold in the late nineteenth century, with just a few of the original collection being returned shortly before the George Harrison photo-shoot. During his life George Harrison became fascinated with the history of the gardens and Sir Frank Crisp, even recording the *Ballad of Sir Frank Crisp* as a tribute. George Harrison was himself a passionate and very talented gardener, and a garden in memory of his life was created for the Royal Horticultural Society Flower Show at Chelsea in 2008. Sadly it did not include any of the gnomes (they are banned from the RHS Chelsea shows), and so they had to stay at home in the gardens at Friar Park.

The inclusion of the Friar Park gnomes on the album cover of *All Things Must Pass* is not the only connection between rock music and gnomes. In 1968 David Bowie recorded 'The Laughing Gnome', perhaps more redolent of the psychedelic gnome than the garden variety.

Stoke Park (now Stoke Pavilions) at Stoke Bruerne in Northamptonshire lies only seventeen miles from Lamport Hall, and here too there were gnomes. A photograph of Stoke in about 1905 shows a group of large gnomes (about 2 feet high) relaxing next to the classical Italianate pool. One is fishing

The gnomes at Stoke Park. Although only a few miles from Lamport Hall no direct connection between the two gnome homes has been found. The Stoke Park gnomes are of the larger type.

in the still waters; another lies on his side, appearing to watch the clouds overhead; the rest stand on the wide gravel path. In the foreground stands a whiskered gnome surrounded by a set of bowls on a flat piece of ground, presumably an old bowling green. All wear the traditional pointed hat and some have the fragile long white clay pipe that so rarely survives. The group looks especially incongruous amongst the combined Jacobean and Palladian splendour of the house and associated pavilions. A second photograph in private archives shows an extra gnome.

Northamptonshire appears to have been a hotbed of gnomes in the nineteenth century, as a further early gnome was recorded in the garden of the Badcock family in Walgrave. Mrs Theodosia Badcock, wife of the retired vicar, was inspired by the collections of Sir Charles Isham to acquire her own German gnome. The gnome lived in the garden of their converted farmhouse in Walgrave and became a firm favourite of their young grandson, who regarded the extremely well made gnome with great fondness. Arriving for family get-togethers he would rush out into the garden to see if the gnome was still there, and to discover what seasonal delights the gardener had placed in the gnome's wheelbarrow (apples, leaves, grass and so on). Many years later both gnome and small boy are retired, but still live happily together in a new garden site. The gnome wears rather distinctive shorts or pantaloons under his smock style jacket, and has traces of paint on the once distinctive red hat.

Gnomes were obviously not restricted to Northamptonshire. Iffley Priory in Oxfordshire was the home of a group of distinctively large gnomes.

Above: This well-travelled German gnome spent his younger days in Walgrave and his middle age in Cornwall, but has now retired to Winchester. Traces of his original paintwork can still be seen.

Left: Iffley Priory gnomes in c.1912, captured by Henry Taunt.

25

Not far from Iffley, a group of much smaller gnomes is captured here in the 1920s, disporting themselves around a rectangular raised basin or birdbath at Sturt Farm in Burford (Oxfordshire).

Captured by the photographer Henry W. Taunt on a sunny summer's day in 1912, the four gnomes inhabited the rich lawns and herbaceous borders of this Gothic Revival house. One of the gnomes carries a small landscaping rake, another gnome has a woven basket, the third perches on an ivy-clad fallen log, whilst the final gnome lays on his side on the lawn. Iffley Priory

Gnome with spade, c.1900. This image is somewhat cryptically recorded as 'Ogo Poggo Man in a private garden on the outskirts of Shanklin'.

was used as a school for much of the nineteenth century, and the gnomes must have been introduced in the 1890s or later. The size and fine detailing indicate German origin, and the survival of both basket and rake may suggest they were relatively recent acquisitions when the photograph was taken.

Sepia toned photographs of nineteenth- and early twentieth-century gnomes can be found in archives and museums all over the country, but all too often with no record of which garden they were photographed in. A typical example is a photograph of a large garden gnome, equipped with European style spade, posed in a rockery or fernery. Thought to date from around 1900, there is no indication of which garden he is in, although the scale suggests something larger than a suburban rockery.

More easily located is the gnome shown on the balcony gardens of the famous property now known as '78 Derngate'. In 1916–17 the distinctive house and interior was re-modelled for Wenman Joseph Bassett-Lowke by Charles Rennie Mackintosh. By the 1920s a gnome lurked on the balcony of Number 78, a slightly odd note against the restrained colours and lines of the Rennie Mackintosh design. Other garden gnomes made their home in Bassett-Lowke's next house, New Ways. New Ways was also the result of collaboration between owner and designer, in this case Peter Behrens. In the 1920s Whynne Bassett-Lowke used to move the gnomes around the garden during the night so that when the younger members of the family came to stay they would play 'hunt the gnome'. It was a rather odd clash of styles in what has been described as the first ever Modern Movement house in England. The gnomes at Derngate and New Ways appear to have had their origins in Germany and may have been collected personally by Whynne Bassett-Lowke on his frequent trips to Germany on business.

Perhaps the 'stateliest' of gnomes were those especially flown out to decorate the lawns of 'Woodside' in Long Island in preparation for a visit by the then Prince of Wales in the 1920s. The gnomes apparently originated in Wales, perhaps accounting for their rather unorthodox appearance in comparison to other gnomes of the period. On hearing of the impending visit of the prince, the gnomes had been hastily acquired by Mr and Mrs James A. Burden of Syosset, Long Island. The prince was undoubtedly over for the polo for which Woodside is famous, and his hosts were said to be anxious to provide 'a home atmosphere', replete with gnomes. It is doubtful

This view of the distinctive modernist architecture of 78 Derngate (Northampton) contains a gnome in the right-hand corner of the second-floor balcony.

The well-travelled 'royal' Welsh gnomes pictured at their new home in Long Island, USA.

whether the prince realised that 'his' gnomes were in a similar pose to those at the public gardens on the Isle of Wight!

Garden gnomes made what was to be a unique appearance at the first ever Chelsea Flower Show just before the First World War. The then 'Great

Gnomes at the International Horticultural Exhibition, held at Chelsea in 1912.

Spring Show' had been held at different venues until 1912, when circumstances dictated that the International Horticultural Exhibition that year should be held at the Chelsea venue. Orchestrated by the nurseryman Harry Veitch, the exhibition had stands by some of the most famous seeds suppliers and nurseries of the period. In amongst these was the Carter's Seeds stand, and featured at the front of the Carter's stand were gnomes. These were not small porcelain miniature figures but the larger style of gnome, bearing baskets of flowers between their hoary hands. A very traditional gnome with the distinctive pointed hat was joined by two rather less distinguished gnomes. Although equipped with beards and jackets, these had the rather more battered hats reminiscent of a down-at-heel gardener. Unfortunately the photographs of the occasion were in black and white so the colours of these Edwardian examples remain a mystery.

The gnome or dwarf continued to appear as good luck symbols on Easter and Christmas cards in Germany, Scandinavia, and other central European countries throughout 1900–30. Although not strictly a garden gnome, the idea of the gnome (in fact probably thought of as a dwarf in this context) as a figure bringing luck to the house and garden was reinforced by the appearance of these characters on numerous cards aimed at both adults and, increasingly, children. The association with Easter, Christmas, and the New Year demonstrate the versatility of the figures; it was rather like having Father Christmas turn up to celebrate the summer solstice (and it should be

An early-twentieth-century Austrian Easter card featuring rabbits, eggs and 'gnomes' (or dwarfs).

A 1950s concrete version of the fashionable gnome with rabbit.

remembered that the *nisse* of Denmark had originally included a *Julenisse*, with a remarkable resemblance to Santa Claus). Some manufacturers and sellers of garden gnomes also started to link the gnome with other garden animals, and made and sold rabbits, deer and even tortoises. 'Gnome with rabbit' became a frequent sight in garden figure catalogues.

Gnomes were often seen with musical instruments on greetings cards, and again the idea of the musical dwarf or gnome was later to cross over to the suburban garden gnome, with modern gnomes sporting guitars rather than the more traditional flutes or trumpets. As the fashion for Christmas cards flourished in the late nineteenth and early twentieth century, these figures became a familiar sight across Europe.

Although again not strictly garden gnomes, gnome-like figures also made a brief appearance in the scandal of the Cottingley garden fairies in 1917. This series of photographs supposedly captured real fairies dancing around two sisters in Cottingley, West Yorkshire, and was perhaps the first ever case of photographic manipulation. The fairies were in fact cut outs, but fooled such luminaries of the Edwardian world as Sir Arthur Conan Doyle. Like Sir Frank Crisp, Conan Doyle was a believer in spiritualism and 'little folk', and even claimed that the head of a pin clearly seen protruding from a gnome's stomach in one of the photographs was in fact a navel. Although usually dismissed nowadays, there are still some unsolved mysteries surrounding the case.

The Cottingley 'theme' was also taken up by the well-known amateur photographer, Mrs G. A. Barton. Here the gnomes, appearing to be

This 1920s depiction of a musical group was sent from Schönau in Baden-Württemberg.

extremely high-quality and detailed examples, carried their autumnal gifts of apples and fruits to a young woman seated amongst a riotous display of foxgloves and delphiniums. Photographed just after the First World War, this photograph (see page 18) captures the final years of gnome respectability.

Despite their increasing popularity in England and America, Germany continued to be the real home of gnomes throughout the early twentieth century. During the First World War there appears to have been a German fashion for being photographed with garden gnomes. Whether these were

From the same series comes this (somewhat quieter) Christmas card.

considered good luck charms, harking back to their origins in the mountain heartlands, or whether they were regarded more as mascots, is unknown. Given the setting of the photographs, at least some may be the result of German soldiers being billetted in the sort of upper-class gardens that housed collections of gnomes by this period. In 1918 *The New York Times* had reported on the 'gnomes and hobgoblins' featuring in the shop windows in Cologne and forming part of the 'German traditional Christmas'. As gnome collections in England had in the main been brought back direct from Germany up until this period, they had a strong association with that country, which may well have contributed to the apparently sudden fall in the fashion for gnomes in upper-class English households and gardens in the 1920s.

There was still a small market for upper-class garden gnomes in England in the 1920s and 1930s, when one was included in the catalogue of the garden statuary company H. Crowther Ltd. Established in 1908, the company specialised in stone, terracotta and leadwork, with many items based on

Above: This modern garden gnome (complete with sunglasses) listens to his fellow gnome on the double bass. Other models include guitars and accordions.

Right: A group of German soldiers hold two garden gnomes, amongst other mascots including a dog.

eighteenth-century originals. The garden gnome figure (shown here in a mid-twentieth-century catalogue) was in fact labelled 'dwarf', but displays the typical pointed hat, beard and sideburns, and smiling face. A large gnome, at 2 feet 6 inches, he was apparently modelled on an Austrian or Czech terracotta pattern. For a while the last Crowther gnome lurked in a bookshop in Chiswick, the home of the Crowther firm, but sadly the bookshop closed and the last gnome retired to reside in the Crowther gardens. Crowther no longer sells garden gnomes or, more correctly, dwarfs.

Above: The last lonely Crowther dwarf surrounded by a range of classical lead figures.

Right: The Crowther 'Dwarf' (clearly a garden gnome), from an undated catalogue. The dwarf stands proudly amongst the range of classical figures.

340 FOUNTAIN
"CUPID AND FISH"
Height 1 ft.

341
"CRYING BOY WITH FISH"
Height 1 ft. 5 in.

333 FOUNTAIN
"BOYS AND DOLPHIN"
Height 2 ft. 9 in.

*523 WATTEAU FIGURES
Height 3 ft.
Pair

322 "DWARF"
Height 2 ft. 6 in.

Note.—Bases are in Stone or Artificial Stone unless otherwise stated.
* Bases are not included in price.

GNOMES IN SUBURBIA

EVEN BEFORE the close of the nineteenth century gnomes were teetering on the fickle knife-edge of taste. Whilst the Lamport Hall rockery took pride of place in an article on the gardens in *Country Life*, the gardening writer of the same magazine was busy explaining in another piece 'what to avoid in a rock garden'. He ruled that 'miserable statuettes, nose-less or otherwise mutilated, are abominations'. It is not clear if his judgement included garden gnomes with unmutilated noses, but one suspects so. Their fall from serious horticultural favour was confirmed by the specific prohibition of gnomes from the Royal Horticultural Society Chelsea Flower Show, along with 'highly coloured figures, fairies or any similar creatures, actual or mythical, as garden ornaments'.

Few 'stately gnome' photographs survive from the inter-war period. Perhaps their owners were aware of the unpopular link with Germany and their use as mascots for some German soldiers, or perhaps it was simply that the opportunities for collecting gnomes direct from the German heartlands had passed, and the fashion passed with them. By the 1930s, gnomes in England were increasingly seen as suited more to suburban lawns and amusement parks than stately homes; their cheery faces began to be associated with seaside outings and children's amusements rather than country house pools and stately rockeries. In his influential work, *Garden Decoration and Ornament for Smaller Houses*, garden designer Geoffrey Jellicoe recorded the work-yards of the many garden firms of the 1930s as 'filled with hundreds of figures, ranging from birdbaths to gnomes and dwarfs', now predominantly manufactured in cement. But these hundreds of gnomes and dwarfs were not the garden ornaments that Jellicoe recommended to his readers. 'Gnomes and things', he stated, are mainly of poor design because they do not have 'the strength of sculptural modelling to enforce their argument'. They did not have those essentials that Jellicoe required of garden ornaments: 'good quality and stimulation of literary imagination'. By the 1930s, gnomes were to be restricted to suburban gardens and public parks.

The famous Blackgang Chine Gardens, first created in the 1840s to take advantage of the increasing number of holidaymakers on the Isle of Wight coast, gained a Gnome Garden in 1934. The gnome garden was created by

Opposite:
A model windmill also looms large over these gnomes in the famous rock garden at New Romney railway station in the 1950s. The Romney, Hythe and Dymchurch miniature railway in Kent was popular with holidaymakers and the rock garden gave it the air of a large scale suburban garden or holiday park.

the owner Bruce Dabell 'as a reflection of the garden fashions in suburbia' at the time. Dabell imported the gnomes from Germany, including a mix of the traditional pointed-hat gnome, the 'Tyrolean hat' gnome and the gnome with slouchy hat, but all wore the regulation waistcoat and beard. This most famous gnome garden consisted of scenes or tableaux of gnomes of typically bright colours grouped with other creatures such as frogs, rabbits and a tortoise (although photographs of the period make it difficult to establish whether the tortoise was artificial or just slow moving). The main tableau comprised a trio of gnomes playing cards on a large toadstool. This card-playing motif was something that had been seen in earlier dwarf postcards and pictures, and appears to have been a popular addition to the original gardening gnome. Over the years the playing cards seem to have been variously stolen and replaced, but in the original scene one gnome is laying an ace. Others of a much smaller size sheltered under other fungi, or climbed up into a miniature raised log cabin. The difference in scale of the figures was not seen as a problem in the composition.

Dabell and his descendants also sold gnomes from the gift shop at the gardens, originally importing these too from Germany, but later on buying from the home market and cheaper imports. The Blackgang Chine Gnome Garden remains a popular attraction in 2009, and money thrown into the well in the tableau is donated to cancer charities. Due to the erosion of the nearby cliffs the Gnome Garden has been relocated several times over the years, but still includes some of the originals. Other early public gardens incorporating gnome scenes included that at St Agnes in Cornwall.

Inspired by the 1937 Disney film *Snow White and the Seven Dwarfs*, which had been popular throughout the Second World War, gnomes took on a new lease of life in the post-austerity period. Sometimes even accompanied by a Snow White, the seven gem-mining dwarfs of Disney's imagination became popular patterns for garden gnomes. On occasions a Bambi or Thumper

The Gnome Garden at Blackgang Chine in the 1930s. The postcard refers to this group as 'smugglers'.

As time passed, the playing cards went missing but the gnomes stayed.

would wander in from another Disney classic to keep the gnomes company, creating early versions of Disneyland on suburban front lawns. The deer also recalled the earlier forest settings of the gnomes' homeland.

Concrete gnomes were responsible for the mass market in gnomes, being easy and relatively quick to produce from moulds and considerably cheaper than hand-modelled pieces. Costs were initially kept relatively high due to the need for hand painting. Their detailing was frequently poor: some had visible

Bottom left: Photographs of gnomes are being discovered all the time, but often there is little information about them. The style of the gnomes and the casual appearance of the man suggest that this photograph may have been taken in a public garden in the 1930s or 1950s. The gnomes are large, but appear to have relatively little detail.

Below: A 1947 'Doc' gnome based on the character in the Disney film of *Snow White and the Seven Dwarfs*.

air bubbles from the manufacturing process and the facial characteristics were basic. The date of the earliest concrete gnomes is not known, but by the post-war period they were the most commonly available type until the heyday of the plastic gnome.

Gnomes that continued to be made in ceramics were also often considerably less detailed than their nineteenth-century forebears. Politely termed 'naively modelled' gnomes of this type range from extremely poor to quite attractive. For example the Lauterbach gnomes made by Hans Groth in Lauterbach (in the Hesse region of Germany) were carefully painted if simplistic. However, many of the products of factories set up in East

EMESS QUALITY GARDEN ORNAMENTS

GF20 Retail 33/6 Trade 16/8 Pur. Tax 8/6   GF30 Retail 31/11 Trade 15/8 P. Tax 8/3   GF35 Retail 29/9 Trade 14/8 P. Tax 7/9   GF40 Retail 31/9 Trade 15/8 P. Tax 8/3

GF55 Retail 37/11 Trade 18/8 P. Tax 9/11   GF60 Retail 37/11 Trade 18/8 P. Tax 9/11   GF10 Retail 33/6 Trade 16/8 Pur. Tax 8/6

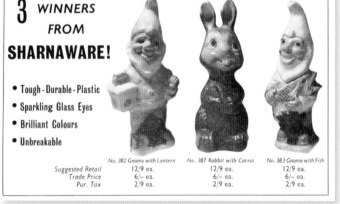

3 WINNERS FROM SHARNAWARE!

- Tough - Durable - Plastic
- Sparkling Glass Eyes
- Brilliant Colours
- Unbreakable

	No. 382 Gnome with Lantern	No. 387 Rabbit with Carrot	No. 383 Gnome with Fish
Suggested Retail	12/9 ea.	12/9 ea.	12/9 ea.
Trade Price	6/– ea.	6/– ea.	6/– ea.
Pur. Tax	2/9 ea.	2/9 ea.	2/9 ea.

These Sharnaware English plastic gnomes were recommended as being unbreakable, and were also much cheaper than the Emess Quality Garden Gnomes advertised on the same page. However, they were also lacking in detail.

Germany, Poland and Czechoslovakia produced gnomes that were extremely poorly moulded and of a cheap fabric. Bulk road transport made heavy concrete gnomes an option and imports dominated the market.

An exception to this general simplification of features can be found in the gnomes produced by Kurt Renno, known as 'Reju' gnomes. The small Reju gnome workshop in Ransbach, in Westerwald in Germany, operated in the 1950–65 period producing detailed gnomes in heavy red clay. It is intriguing to consider that whilst Renno was working away handmoulding his red clay gnomes, the large company of Plachy and Materene was turning out endless plastic gnomes just a few miles away in the town of Wirges, also in Westerwald. Trading as 'Puma' plastics, the firm rose high on the boom in hard plastics, producing a huge range of gnomes and other figures (including one looking suspiciously like Snow White, and another rather incongruously wearing a sheriff's badge). Plachy and Materene also made ceramics, but it was the moulded plastic that travelled best, and their business prospered on an active export trade as well as in the West German market, despite competition from East Germany.

Westerwald was something of a Mecca for gnomes in the 1950s, as the Spang Gnome Company was also based there. Clemens Spang started gnome manufacturing in the 1950s, using earthenware, but with a combination of spray painting and hand painting. The gnomes were vividly 'craggy' in their depiction and unlike many of the plastic gnomes of the period, neither cute nor chubby. The Spang catalogue was also unusual, with line and ink drawings of the various types of gnome available making the catalogue itself appear home made.

It was the 1950s that saw gnomes change forever. The advent of plastics meant that gnomes could be created in glorious technicolour as cheap and cheerful additions to any garden, no matter how small. Although plastic gnomes had the disadvantage of being less detailed than even their concrete cousins, they were weatherproof and largely unbreakable. The chubby cheeks, bulbous noses, and smooth cheery faces took the new generation of garden gnomes even farther away from the original figures modelled on 'real' little folk. The simplicity of modelling of these plastic gnomes was part of their endearing nature, a fortunate side effect of low standards of plastic moulding in this early period. Gradually this 'simpler' type of gnome came to predominate even within the ceramic and concrete gnome manufacturers, who often abandoned earlier costly materials and production methods.

By the 1950s the post-war Disney boom, combined with the low cost of imports and the rise of the garden centre, had resulted in a rash of the new style of gnomes. These were firmly suburban gnomes, bringing bright colours to small patches of lawn. Combined with wishing wells and windmills, they formed truly 'miniature landscapes'. In 1960, *Country Life* ran another article on Lamport Hall. Neglecting to mention their own original role in the promotion of the once famous rockery, the author opined, 'it is to be feared that

Right: This cheerful plastic gnome, set amongst colourful annuals and artificial flowers, is typical of the later twentieth-century image of the gnome.

Far right: A concrete gnome of the 1950s. Rosy-cheeked but still 'life-like'.

the fame of the Lamport rockery towards the end of the nineteenth century was one of the influences that promoted the regrettable over-population of the race from which we now suffer'. It was to be the rise before the fall.

At the same time as they were 'over-populating' the suburbs, gnomes began to be selectively written out of garden history. As the number of books on the history of garden design and garden ornaments grew, so the wall of silence on gnomes thickened. Where gnomes were included, they were invariably treated with contempt. In *English Garden Ornament* (1965), a book by Paul Edwards that gives serious and worthy consideration to such ornaments as rustic seating and shell grottoes, the author describes garden gnomes and their accompanying toadstools as 'making countless front gardens look ridiculous'. The presence of a garden gnome, he said, sacrificed garden design to sentiment. The best one can say of the garden ornament of the suburban garden, he claimed, is 'that it is still a young art'. Obviously the centuries-old heritage of the garden gnome had not attracted his attention. By the 1980s writers on the use of garden

Wells and windmills became popular accoutrements of the garden gnome in the mid twentieth century. This well has recently been given a makeover and its accompanying gnomes carry artificial flowers.

ornamentation were warning their readers specifically against making a gnome garden, although small (classical) figures in plain stone were seen as perfectly acceptable. Peter McHoy even warned of placing herons or frogs on a front lawn where 'they will look like garden gnomes'. By 1989 the garden historian George Plumptre did not mention the gnome in *Garden Ornament*, his broad-ranging history, although he was quite prepared to include 'statues' of squirrels, deer and even a 'classical' snail.

The firm of Harcostar in Huntingdon manufactured plastic gnomes throughout the 1960s and 1970s, bucking a trend by using high-quality materials. Harcostar were predominantly manufacturers of industrial drums and containers and pioneered the use of blow-moulding glass-reinforced materials with EVA (Ethylene Vinyl Acetate). Used on the outside of products, the EVA coating was able to take paint without a primer, whilst on

This continental gnome has a rather up-market windmill residence. Windmills and gnomes were a common sight on the lawns of 1950s suburbia in England.

41

the inside it acted as a barrier to fuel vapour and other chemicals. Unsurprisingly the gnomes were rather a sideline for the company, but were produced with some of the most advanced technology seen in plastic gnomes! Sourcing their moulds from Denmark, the company used high-density polythene as a base material and blended this with reground material and a batch pigment to suit. To minimise the need for painting the gnomes were largely colour-coordinated, with green gnomes boasting green jackets, hats and trousers. The necessary painting was at first carried out on site, but as the quality of the gnomes resulted in higher demand, local outworkers hand-painted the gnomes with acrylic paints similar to those used on the industrial containers made by the company. In the early 1980s these outworkers included the inmates of the local prison at Littlehey. With time on their hands, the prisoners branched out into time-consuming designs such as tartan trousers and check jackets. Despite a media stunt in 1981, when hundreds of Harcostar gnomes were lined up at Huntingdon's railway station, the company stopped making the gnomes (along with the accompanying windmills and garden planters) at some point in the early 1980s.

The firm Major's Garden Ornaments, founded by the father of former British Prime Minister John Major, made its last gnome in 1962, presaging the eventual collapse of the gnome industry. Founded in 1930, it had made a range of colourful gnomes through the worst years of the war and into the years of austerity, but with the advent of 'swinging Britain' the gnome was left homeless and the firm was forced to close. Terry Major Ball (John Major's brother) still continued to collect garden gnomes as souvenirs when travelling in other countries, but the collapse of the family firm suggested that he was in a small minority of gnome fanciers.

These three cheerful Harcostar gnomes still display their original paintwork including the unusual bright yellow dungarees.

The garden gnome was at a low ebb. Vilified by the gardening press, banned from the Royal Horticultural Society portals, and yet to gain an antique value, the future looked bleak. Estate agents even issued advice to prospective house sellers to hide the gnomes when buyers came to call, for fear of lowering the price of the house. A few collections still hung on, clinging to the rocks at places like Blackgang Chine, but their days seemed numbered.

GARDEN ORNAMENTS

Toadstool 3/11	Fisherman 22/6	Mushroom 3/11	Gardener 22/6	Dog 11/3	Woodman 27/6
Digging Hare 11/3	Chubby Gnome 11/3	Sitting Fisherman 14/9	Owl 11/3	Large Hare 11/3
Large Frog 11/3	Medium Rabbit 6/3	Happy Gnome 11/3	Gnome with lantern 7/3	Woodpecker 6/3
Tortoise 11/3	Small Rabbit 2/6	Small Hare 3/9	Small Frog 6/3	Small Duck 2/6

Also available : Stone Tubs, Bird Baths, etc.

Below left:
Although
unpopular amongst
garden historians
and professional
gardeners, in
reality gnomes
were still popular
with the suburban
gardener, as
exemplified by this
1950s advertising
campaign for
ATCO
lawnmowers,
which features
helpful gardening
gnomes.

Above: An advertisement of the early 1960s from the company J. C. Withers. They included in their brochure the range of Snow White dwarfs, as well as more traditional and detailed gnomes.

Below right:
Another ATCO
lawnmower
advertisement.

THE GNOME REBORN

AS SURE AS popularity is followed by decline, so the pendulum swings again, and by the mid 1980s gnomes began to bounce back. This period saw the arrival of the female gnome, the battery-driven gnome and the 'naughty gnome', typically exposing parts of gnomish anatomy not previously included in gnome lore. These gnomes (male and female) started life in central Europe, with many coming from the large cut-price gnome outlets in Poland and Czechoslovakia. Instantly popular in Germany, the naughty gnomes spread into England and eventually America. 'Mooning' gnomes are the most common, but drunken gnomes, naked gnomes (sometimes only retaining the pointed hat) and gnomes in compromising positions can also lurk in the garden. Some firms now specialise in this type of gnome, taking the gnome ethos even farther from the original garden gnome, who was traditionally always seen hard at work, or at most enjoying a leisurely pipe. Sound effects, fitted into resin and plastic gnomes and operated by battery or even solar power, add an unfortunate degree of realism to some of the activities.

By the 1990s the few remaining makers of traditional gnomes were under serious threat from an invasion of cheap gnomes (naughty and otherwise) from Eastern Europe. As the European Union expanded, it was no longer possible to prevent these poor-quality gnomes from crossing the borders into Germany. Once held back by a strict law on copyright, the companies could now copy original designs and make them in cheaper materials, materials which often cracked and peeled with the first frost but which were attractively cheap to purchase. Gnomes were even imported from China and Korea back into the original gnomish heartlands. One estimate put the number of gnomes sold from Polish roadsides and street kiosks near the German border as high as five million, and by 2005 Poland had its own 'Gnome Capital' at Nowa Sol. In 2006 Krzysztof Baczek, based at Nowa Sol, sold 5,000 gnomes a month through his firm Westimex, founded on a capital of £800 and by then worth £3.4 million – a testimony to entrepreneurship and the renewed appeal of the gnome. His resin gnomes sold for less than £5 each in supermarkets and easily undercut the clay hand-painted gnomes still

Opposite:
A gnome caught in the act of bringing a ray of sunshine into a garden.

lovingly produced (and individually named) by the Griebel family.

Of the original manufacturers of the ceramic garden gnome, only a few survived into the 21st century. Heissner, whose founder August Heissner created his first garden gnome in 1872, is now based in Lauterbach. After closing between 1941 and 1944, the company expanded into plastic gnomes during the 1950s, to beat off competition from the USA. Heissner

Above: This mooning gnome is comparatively tasteful given the wide range of other poses now available.

Right: Gnomes waiting to cross the border between Germany and the Czech Republic. Sold by a shop calling itself 'Asia Market', they further confused the gnomish gene pool.

Above left: These gnomes and other characters were captured in a colourful garden near Hamburg, Germany. Numbers of gnomes in Germany remain extremely healthy, with estimates of anything between 4 million and 25 million gnomes living in suburban gardens, allotments, and in 'small garden colonies'.

Above right: The gnomes are also popular in gardens associated with *Kleinegarten* (allotments) and campsites in former East Germany.

now produces a wide range of garden equipment but still prides itself on its gnomes, producing plastic gnomes for the 2006 FIFA World Cup and recently making available a T-shirt emblazoned 'Heissner Gnome Fan'. In Gräfenroda itself, instead of the original sixteen gnome manufacturers, only Griebel survives, specialising in traditionally styled handmade gnomes as well as the increasingly popular 'naughty gnomes'. Outside the German heartland of the gnome, the Silvestri company, based in San Francisco, still makes cast stone gnomes under the fourth generation of Silvestri, with the emphasis on quality and fine detailing, whilst USA-based Brian Kibler has founded the World of Johann Maresch, making new Maresch gnomes by taking moulds from original antiques.

Perhaps the most distinctive gnome maker of the twenty-first century is Candice Kimmel, who classes herself as a gnome artist. Based in the evocative Black Hill area of South Dakota (USA), Kimmel originated in Wales, a region similarly associated with mining. Kimmel uses original eighteenth- and nineteenth-century gnomes as mould patterns for her new creations, and English stoneware fabric gives a quality similar to the original. Hand painted and then re-fired, the gnomes are modern masterpieces, rivalling any nineteenth-century example in quality and detail.

Not all twenty-first century gnomes are distinguished by their artistic detail. Continued use of plastics allows a wider range of poses and clothing than ever before, and design and manufacture of 'short runs' for topical events has never been easier. During the 2006 World Cup a range of football action gnomes in the national team colours proved so popular that a leading supermarket chain claimed it was selling one every five seconds. As well as footballing gnomes, the 1980s saw the appearance of the political gnome and satirical gnome: first Margaret Thatcher gnomes and then Tony Blair gnomes with extended ears – a sort of Tony Blair meets Mr Spock. Despite the family connections with gnome making, there does not appear ever to have been a John Major gnome.

Far right: One of the several gnomes from antique moulds being manufactured and offered by Kimmel Gnomes.

Right: 'Archibald' Gnome has also been created by Kimmel from original German moulds.

Kimmel has also created a range of 'modern' gnomes with distinctively tall pointy hats and round jolly faces.

The largest makers of concrete gnomes in England today are Whelan's of Kent. They sell mainly through garden centres and carry a range of 'traditional' style gnomes, with wheelbarrows and watering cans in hand, as well as *Snow White and the Seven Dwarfs* groups, and the inevitable musical gnome and gnome with deer or snail. Plastic and resin gnomes are largely imported from China; Silver Lynx Products exported over 10,000 in 1997. The use of plastic resin with bonded colour (reminiscent of the work of Harcostar) allows a wide range of colours and styles at a price to encourage impulse purchase.

One of the most telling signs of the gnome revival was the start of an active market in antique gnomes, with a brief flurry of interest at Sotheby's, as well as a more sustained interest on the rather less prestigious eBay. The web-based gnome fan site and outlet, Gnomeland, has compiled a list of auction prices for gnomes from 2006 onwards, listing manufacturer, material and approximate date of manufacture. Passing through the auctioneers' hands from 2006 onwards were vintage terracotta gnomes, 1950s gnomes in plastic and resin, late-nineteenth-century gnomes from their homelands of Thuringia, gnomes by makers such as Griebel, Heissner and Spang, gnomes with rakes, gnomes with rabbits, and gnomes with fishing rods. For the gnome collectors, rarity is prized over any particular garden style and prices for early gnomes have escalated. In October 2006, a rare German garden gnome dating from before 1900 sold for almost £600. Made of terracotta on a wooden core, he stood over 24 inches tall, but had unfortunately lost his wheelbarrow over the years, leaving him grasping the empty air. A few years later a German terracotta gnome from the early 1900s changed hands for around £2,000, and a simple fishing gnome was sold at Sotheby's for £391.

A modern resin gnome retains its gardening credentials despite mass production.

Not just the garden gnomes themselves but also garden gnome 'ephemera' now attract attention. Early photographs of gnomes *in situ*, manufacturers' catalogues of garden gnomes, postcards with gnomes on, even gnome moulds, all have a brisk market in auction houses and on the web.

The gnome revival has also seen the setting up of 'gnome reserves' and museums around the world, often combining collections of antique gnomes with displays of more recent gnomes grouped in their traditional garden settings. Griebels have a museum on site housing their own historic gnomes and documenting their early-nineteenth-century history, whilst the town of Gräfenroda advertises itself as the home of the gnome. The Gnome Reserve in North Devon welcomes all gnomes, traditional or modern. Opened in 1979 by artist Ann Atkin, in the 1980s it had as many as 30,000 visitors a year, who came

A rosy-cheeked garden gnome such as this early 1950s example might find himself highly valued one day in the increasingly popular gnome-collectors market. In the meantime he has much sentimental value for his present owner.

to see the seventy gnomes within the museum and the collection of over a thousand modern gnomes spread throughout the 4-acre grounds. Still a favourite tourist destination in 2008, visitors are 'encouraged' to wear complementary red pointed hats whilst they tour the gnomes, and fishing rods can be loaned out if you really want to get into the full feel of the part. In common with Sir Charles Isham, Ann Atkin believes in the creative and spiritual power of the gnome, casting a spell on your subconscious and connecting earth and heaven. Similar gnome reserves and 'open garden' collections exist in the USA and the Netherlands and even in Australia, where a free-ranging community of over a thousand gnomes appeared on a roundabout at Wellington Mills (West Australia). 'Gnomesville' is now a tourist destination in its own right, despite vandalism reducing the gnome numbers during 'The Gnomesville Massacre' in 2007. Underwater gnome gardens are perhaps the most unusual modern 'twist' on the story of the garden gnome, with the creation of a gnomery in Lake Wastwater, Cumbria. 'Gnomes in Space' must surely follow soon.

A less successful venture was the gnomery based at the famous Edwardian Rock garden in Aysgarth (Yorkshire). Originally created for local plantsman and furrier Frank Sayer-Graham, the enormous rock garden was painstakingly put together by the firm of James Backhouse & Son in the years between 1906 and 1912. By the mid twentieth century the rock garden had fallen into decay and a new owner, determined to turn it into a money-making venture, peopled the rocks with gnomes, combining tourist attraction with gnome shop. Alas, the venture came just before the gnome revival and the rock garden was doomed to fall yet again into decay and disrepair until its recognition as a historic feature in the late 1980s and subsequent restoration. During the restoration numerous small fragments of gnomes were found, testimony to the combined efforts of the previous owner

Tony Blair gnome, now retired and living at the Museum of Garden History, London.

and the prowess of the local youths with their air rifles. The current owners are anxious to maintain the original atmosphere of the Edwardian garden, but have allowed some of the 1980s gnomes to creep back in.

Away from his natural habitat, the garden gnome has also made a surprising cultural comeback, appearing in films, television and advertising campaigns as well as dedicated websites. In 1997 the hit movie *The Full Monty* was the first to boast a 'gnome scene'. In the scene one of the characters is distracted during a job interview by his friends, who stage a garden gnome battle outside the window behind the interviewer's head, with predictable impact on his interview performance. This cameo role for the garden gnome was followed by a more substantial appearance in the 2001 French film *Amélie*. Concerned about her stay-at-home father, Amélie kidnaps her father's gnome and arranges for it to be sent around the world, posing against backdrops of world-famous sights. Holiday snaps accompanied by appropriate greetings are sent back to her father. On his eventual return, the well-travelled gnome eventually inspires her father to take off on global adventures. Similar real and fictional cases of gnome-gnapping inspired the travel website Travelocity to use their 'roaming gnome' in a series of advertisements. A website was set up to follow the movements of the roaming gnome (www.whereismygnome.com), making the campaign a household name. The original real-life roaming gnome has passed into legend. The contenders for first roaming gnome are an Australian gnome called Bilbo who left his family home in Sydney and sent a postcard from Queensland in the mid 1980s, and a gnome called Bobby.

The success of the $80 million Travelocity campaign inspired other companies, and shortly afterwards the English clothing company Boden ran a 'Gname our Gnome' competition, the winning entry of which was 'Baden Trowel'; a clever play on the boy scout founder, Baden Powell, and the garden digging propensities of the traditional garden gnome, combined with the name Boden. Aiming at a somewhat different consumer market, the clothes company Firetrap has used unusual gnome images to advertise the company since 2003. Building on the ancient mischief-making character of the original dwarf or gnome, they launched Deadly as the first Firetrap gnome and he has since been followed by Deadly Greed, Wrath of Deadly, Summer Lust, Deadly Vanity, Deadly Envy, and Deadly Sloth, each in their own specific colours and facial patterns. The videos and advertising campaigns that accompany them are not for the faint-hearted.

Deadly Envy, a sinister gnome that glows green in the dark, was used to launch the 2007 Firetrap collection of clothes

The Aysgarth Edwardian rock garden still houses a few of the numerous gnomes housed there in the 1980s.

Alton Towers, the Staffordshire theme park, rather inadvertently used gnomes to advertise its attractions in the summer of 2005. Upset by the publication of a book on unusual and traditional attractions in England, which praised attractions such as Gnome Magic and the Gnome Reserve and criticised theme parks, the management at Alton Towers offered free entry to anyone accompanied by a gnome. The offer backfired on them when they found many of their visitors left behind the gnome that they had arrived with, creating a 'gnome mountain' of over 200 gnomes. Tactfully described as gnomes 'forgotten after the thrill of the day', staff at the theme park set up a 'gnome crèche' where people needing a gnome might come and 'rescue' one. The gnome mountain itself spurred a series of articles in newspapers serving as a further advertising impetus, but creating a sad picture of the mistreatment of the garden gnome in the modern day.

In the art world, the French designer Philippe Starck designed a gnome table as part of his new range of indoor furnishing in *c.*2000. Known for his witty design style, the gnome was deliberately modelled on the appearance of the later plastic or cement gnomes, with technicolour features, stubby hands and bright pink cheeks.

Philippe Starck gnome table or stool, *c.* 2000.

Kidnapping or stealing gnomes, sometimes known as 'gnome hunting' or simply 'gnoming', has also become a popular pastime. Sometimes the gnomes are never heard of again, but in other cases owners receive ransom notes or clues to the whereabouts of the roaming gnomes, echoing the exploits in *Amélie*. France and Italy both have websites dedicated to the liberation of gnomes (the *Front de Libération des Nains de Jardins* and the *MALAG* respectively). An American version, the Garden Gnome Liberation

Using gnomes or elves to advertise clothing has a long established history and elves have a particular link to boot manufacture and tailoring. This trade card of c.1880–90 uses elves or gnomes to help advertise its stock of boots. The USA-based company printed its literature in English and German, and the German link may explain the presence of the pointy hats. (Vernor's Ginger Ale of Detroit, Michigan, also used a gnome to advertise their products from at least the early twentieth century, the link supposedly being that the gnome guarded the underground cellars of ale.)

Front (GGLF) calls for 'an end to oppressive gardening and freedom for garden gnomes everywhere'. The website includes instructions on what to do if you find a gnome being held in captivity, and a downloadable letter to send to the person responsible for holding the gnome in slavery. Banning

The modern garden gnome has a choice of hat colours, with green as one of the most popular. Note the female gnomes on the shelf below.

imports of British gnomes and releasing gnomes into the wild are also advocated, along with gnome trafficking embargoes. Satirical in style and content, these websites have actually given rise to cases of gnome-gnapping and theft both in Europe and America, ironically usually of the cheaper colourful front garden gnomes rather than the more valuable antique gnomes, which are usually kept out of sight or indoors. In August 2008 the *Daily Express* reported on a strange finding of a circle of gnomes within woodland near Fishburn, Co. Durham. Lit by a generous complement of solar powered garden lights, the gnomes formed a weird woodland tableau. The gnomes had been stolen from gardens in the area, and after being rescued all but three gnomes and a ceramic toadstool were reclaimed. Locals fear that kidnapping for pagan rites may now be added to the concerns of gnome owners everywhere. In Germany thieves targeted a gnome peepshow where scantily clad gnomes were to be viewed in compromising poses. The owner of the (adults only) amusement park told police, 'I doubt they're standing in someone's garden, they'll have to be hidden inside'. Meanwhile an offshoot of the gnome liberation movement has begun the liberation of plastic flamingos – one suspects windmills will be next.

Even children's books have begun to reflect an increased interest in the garden gnome. Young readers are thrilled by the exploits of *Ned the Gnome*, including a rather touching storyline in which Ned meets almost Zen-like garden gnomes endlessly guarding a miniature fishpond. For older readers the slightly more sinister garden gnomes of the *Goosebumps* series have become popular. These gnomes come to life to create mischief, destruction, and even the threat of death. In so many children's books there is an element of danger lurking beneath even the jauntiest red hat and white beard. Perhaps the original taciturn nature of the dwarf/gnome, as described by Paracelsus in the sixteenth century, has remained with them through the centuries. The BBC has introduced a children's cartoon called *Gordon the Garden Gnome* in an effort to encourage young children to engage with gardening, nature and vegetables. The voice of Gordon is provided by Alan Titchmarsh, the nation's favourite gardener – definitely a cheerful gnome rather than a gruff dwarf! Gordon has become so successful that the Royal Botanic Gardens at Kew have printed Gordon the Gnome information leaflets and themed trails aimed at the 2- to 6-year-old visitors, and Gordon became international when the series was shown on America's Cartoon Network.

Almost 150 years after their introduction into England, garden gnomes are here to stay and appear to be reproducing. Gnomes are now available in a wider range of materials, styles, poses and positions than Sir Charles Isham could ever have dreamt of (or indeed have wished for). In 2007 a traditional garden gnome, complete with white beard, red hat and blue jacket, was finally smuggled into the RHS Chelsea Flower Show by a reporter from the BBC's *Today* programme, and photographed with the horticultural exhibits. The gate-crashing gnome was a protest about the exclusion of these important garden figures with their long pedigree and cheerful outlook from the most prestigious of flower shows. Meanwhile Kew has started to stock gnomes in its garden shop – albeit in alarmingly modern colours. Surely it is only a matter of time before the garden gnome is once again recognised not only for its distinguished history, but also as the essential elemental figure that will bring good luck and success to any garden.

Below: Patiently awaiting repair and rehabilitation and coming soon to a garden near you!

Below right: A row of garishly coloured gnomes awaiting new homes, on sale at the Royal Botanic Gardens, Kew.

BIBLIOGRAPHY

Dohna, Countess U. *Private Gardens of Germany.* Weidenfeld and Nicolson, 1986. (The entry for the Hofgarten at Oettingen includes a consideration of the origin of German *Zwergen-Figuren*).

Edwards, P. *English Garden Ornament.* G. Bell & Sons, 1965.

Egleton, M. *Gnomeland: An Introduction to the World of the Little People.* Kyle Cathie, 2007.

Elliott, B. 'Gnomenclature' in *The Garden*, April issue, 1992, pp.172–5.

Jellicoe, G.A. *Garden Decoration and Ornament for Smaller Houses.* Country Life Ltd, 1936.

Oswald, A. 'The gardens at Lamport Hall' (parts I and II) in *Country Life*, 10 and 17 November, 1960.

Pratt, H. 'A wonderful rock garden' in *The Strand Magazine*, 1890, pp.225–30.

Russell, V. *Gnomes.* Frances Lincoln, 2004.

WEBSITES AND GNOME BLOGS

www.gnomeland.co.uk

www.zwergen-griebel.de (Website of the Griebel gnome manufacturer and gnome museum).

www.heissner.de (Website of the Heissner Company, including a catalogue of their currently available gnomes.)

www.asilvestri.com (Website of the Silvestri company, based in San Francisco, with their stone-cast gnome collection.)

www.zwerglignomes.com (Histories, gallery and gnome shop.)

www.flnjfrance.com (Website of the *Front de Liberation des Nains de Jardins*)

www.freethegnomes.com (Website of the American Garden Gnome Liberation Front)

www.gnutty4gnomes.blogspot.com (Beth Sanderson's daily gnome blog USA)

home.earthlink.net/~artifactsco/maresch (The World of Johann Maresch)

Road sign: beware of gnomes!

INDEX